Exploring Standard Materials in 3ds Max® 2016

Raavi O'Connor

Exploring Standard Materials in 3ds Max® 2016

3ds Max is the registered trademarks of Autodesk Inc.

Book Code: V003C

ISBN: 978-1515165477

http://raavidesign.blogspot.co.uk

Contents

Acknowledgements

About the Author

Preface

C-Hands-on Exercises

Other books from Raavi Design

This page is intentionally left blank

Acknowledgements

Thanks to:

Sarah O'Connor for the cover art and other promotional material.
Alex for formatting the book.
Everyone at Autodesk [www.autodesk.com].

Thanks to all great digital artists who inspire us with their innovative VFX, gaming, animation, and motion graphics content.

And a very special thanks to everyone who helped me along the way in my life and carrier.

Finally, thank you for picking up the book.

This page is intentionally left blank

About the Author

Raavi Design, founded by Raavi O'Connor, is a group of like-minded professionals and freelancers who are specialized in advertising, graphic design, web design and development, digital marketing, multimedia, exhibition, print design, branding, and CG content creation.

At Raavi Design we strive to share the enthusiasm and ideas with other digital artists and provide quality CG content to the aspiring artists and students. Our books are written in an easy to understand language so that the users learn the complex concepts quickly.

The main features of our books are as follows:

- Nicely formatted content in books
- Less theory more practical approach saves you hours of struggle and pain
- Content written in easy to understand language
- Exercises/Labs for practice
- Free updates and exclusive bonus content
- Video tutorials
- Free textures, background design, and 3D files

Here's the list of training books that Raavi has put together:

- The Tutorial Bank: 3D, VFX, & Motion Graphics
- Build Studio Light Setup using 3ds Max and VRay
- Exploring Standard Materials in 3ds Max 2015
- Exploring Standard Materials in 3ds Max 2016
- Exploring Utilities Nodes In Maya 2016 [Coming Soon]
- Create Backgrounds, Textures, and Maps in Photoshop: Using Photoshop CC 2014
- Beginner's Guide To Mental Ray and Autodesk Materials In 3ds Max 2016
- Beginner's Guide For Creating 3D Models In 3ds Max 2016 [Coming Soon]

You can follow **Raavi O'Conner** on Twitter @raavidesign.

Preface

Why this Book?

This book is aimed at those digital artists who have just started working on the 3ds Max. In this book, I have covered standard and related materials as well as the standard maps. A better understanding of materials and maps gives you ability to add realism to your artwork. The concepts you will learn using this book will help you a lot when you will start working on advanced materials such as **VRay** and **mental ray** materials.

This book is written in an easy to understand language. The important terms are in bold face so that you never miss them. This book is written using 3ds Max 2016.

What You Will Learn?

You will learn how to use standard maps with standard and related materials to model realistic looking surfaces. The parameters are explained with examples and related screen captures. Additional tips, guidance, and advice is provided in from of Tips, Notes, and Warnings. You will gain skills by completing the hands-on exercises provided in the Section C of the book.

What you need?

To complete the examples and hands-on exercises in this book, you need v2016 of Autodesk 3ds Max. To know more about these products from Autodesk, visit the following links:

3ds Max: *http://www.autodesk.com/products/3ds-max/overview*

If you are an educator or student, you access free Autodesk software from the **Autodesk Education Community**. The **Autodesk Education Community** is an online resource with more than five million members that lets educators and students to download free Autodesk software. In addition, you can connect with millions of other digital artists to know about latest and greatest in the CG industry.

What are the main features of the book?

- All standard and related materials as well as the standard maps explained.
- 9 examples and 4 hands-on exercises to hone your skills.
- Additional tips, guidance, and advice are provided.
- Important terms are in bold face so that you never miss them.
- Support for technical aspect of the book.
- 3ds Max files and textures used are available for download.

How This Book Is Structured?

This book is organized to provide you with the knowledge needed to master the standard materials and related maps. This book is divided into three sections:

Section A - Standard and Related Materials

The section will guides you through the **Standard** material and related materials such as **Blend**, **Composite**, **Raytrace**, **Multi/Sub-Object** and so forth. The examples used in the section allow you to grasp the concept explained.

Section B - Standard Maps

Autodesk 3ds Max offers many map types that you can use to enhance the look of the material. This section provides an overview of the **Standard** maps.

Section C - Hands-on Exercises

In this section, you will work on the hands-on exercises using the concepts and techniques learned in the book.

Resources

This book is sold via multiple sales channels. If you don't have access to the resources used in this book, you can place a request for the resources by visiting the following link: *http://bit.ly/rd-contact*. Please mention **"Resources - VOO8C"** in the subject line.

Customer Support

At Raavi Design we believe support is personal. Our technical team is always ready to take care of your technical queries. If you have any problem with the technical aspect of the book, navigate to *http://bit.ly/rd-contact* and let us know about your query. Please mention **"Technical Query - VOO8C"** in the subject line. We will do our best to resolve your queries.

Reader Feedback

Your feedback is always welcome. Your feedback is critical to our efforts at Raavi Design and it will help us in developing quality titles in the future. To send the feedback, visit *http://bit.ly/rd-contact*. Please mention **"Feedback - VOO8C"** in the subject line.

Errata

We take every precaution while preparing the content of the book but mistakes do happen. If you face a mistake in this book general or technical, we would be happy that you report it to us so that we can mention it in the errata section of the book's online page. If you find any errata, please report them by visiting the following link: *http://bit.ly/rd-contact*. Please mention "Errata - VOO8C" in the subject line.

This will help the other readers from frustration. Once your errata is verified, it will appear in the errata section of the book's online page.

Stay Connected

Stay connected with us through Twitter (**@raavidesign**) to know the latest updates about our products, information about books, and other related information.

A - Standard and Related Materials

The **Standard** material and related materials such as **Raytrace** material, **Matte/Shadow** material, **Compound** material, and **Ink 'n Paint** material are non-photometric. Do not use these materials if you plan to create physically accurate lighting models. However, these materials are suitable for games, films, and animation. In this section, we are going to look at the standard materials.

Standard Material

The **Standard** material is a straight forward method for modeling surfaces that reflect light. You can use this material to model the reflective properties of a surface. If you don't use 2D or 3D maps with this material, it generates a single uniform color for the surface.

A surface having a single color reflects many other colors such as ambient, diffuse, and specular. The **Standard** materials use a four-color model to simulate the reflected colors from a surface. However, there may be variations depending on the shader you use. The **Ambient** color appears where surface is lit (the surface in the shadow) by the ambient light only. The **Diffuse** color appears on the surface when the lights falls directly on it. The term **Diffuse** is used because light is reflected in various directions. The **Specular** color appears in the highlights. **Highlights** are reflection of light sources on the surface. Generally, shiny surfaces have specular highlights where the viewing angle is equal to the angle of incident. Metallic surfaces show another type of highlights called glancing highlights. The glancing highlights have a high angle of incidence. Some surfaces in the real-world are highly reflective. To model such surfaces, you can use a reflection map or use raytracing. The **Filter** color is the color transmitted through an object. The **Filter** color will only be visible, if **Opacity** is less than **100** percent.

The three color components blend at the edge of their respective regions. The blend of the **Diffuse** and **Ambient** components is controlled by the shader. However, you can control the blending by using the **Standard** material's highlight controls.

To create a **Standard** material, press **M** to open the **Slate Material Editor**. On **Material Editor | Material |Map Browser | Materials | Standard rollout**, double-click **Standard** to add a standard material node to the active view. Figure 1 shows the **Standard** material's interface. If you double-click on the material node, its attributes appear in various rollouts on the **Parameter Editor**. The controls on these rollouts change according to the shader type chosen from the **Shader Basic Parameters** rollout [see Figure 2].

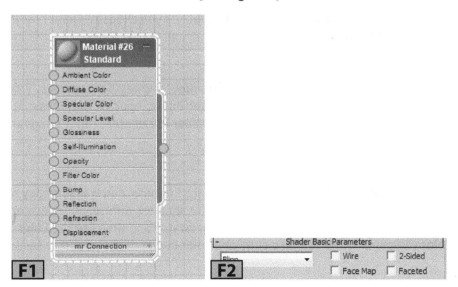

The controls in this rollout let you choose the type of shader to use with the **Standard** material. **Wire** lets you render the material in the wireframe mode [see Figure 3]. You can change the size of the wire using the **Size** control on the material's **Extended Parameters** rollout. Figure 4 shows the render with **Size** set to **2**. **2-Sided** that allows you to make a 2-sided material. When you select this option, 3ds Max applies material to the both sides of the selected faces.

Note: One-sided faces
In 3ds Max, faces are one-sided. The front side is the side with the surface normals. The back side of the faces is invisible to the renderer. If you see this other side from the back, the faces will appear to be missing.

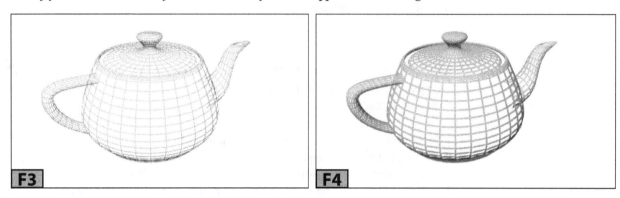

The **Face Map** control allows you to apply the material to the faces of the geometry. If material is a mapped material, it requires no mapping coordinates and automatically applied to each face. Figures 5 and 6 show the render with **Face Map** in off and on states, respectively. The **Faceted** control renders each face of the surface as if it were flat [see Figure 7].

Tip: Rendering both sides of a face
*There are two ways to render both sides of a face. Either you can turn on **Force 2-Sided** in the **Render Setup dialog | Common panel | Options group** or apply a two sided material to the faces.*

The **Shader** drop-down located at the extreme left of the rollout lets you choose a shader for the material. Here's is the quick rundown to the various material shaders:

Phong Shader
You can use this shader to produce realistic highlights for shiny, and regular surfaces. This shader produces strong circular highlights. This shader can accurately render bump, opacity, shininess, specular, and reflection maps. When you select the **Phong** shader, the **Phong Shader Parameters** rollout appears in the material's **Parameter Editor** [see Figure 8].

Phong Shader Parameters Rollout
The controls in this rollout, let you set the color of the material, shininess, and transparency of the material. The **Ambient, Diffuse,** and **Specular** controls let you set the colors for ambient, diffuse, and specular color components, respectively. To change a color component, click on the color swatch and then use the **Color Selector** to change the values of the color component. You can also copy one color component to another by dragging the source

color swatch to the target color swatch. In the **Copy or Swap Colors** dialog, click **Swap**, or **Copy** button. Click **Cancel** to cancel the operation. You can lock or unlock two color components using the **Lock** button [see Figure 9].

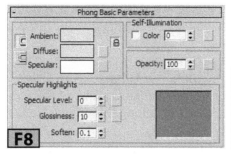
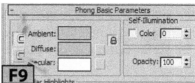

The buttons located on the right of color swatches can be used to apply texture maps to the respective color components. On clicking these buttons, the **Material/Map Browser** appears that allows you to select a map for the color component. If you want to apply different maps to the **Ambient** and **Diffuse** components, click on the **Lock** button located to the right of these components [see Figure 10].

Self-Illumination Group

You can use the controls in this group to make the material self-illuminated. The illusion of self-illumination is created by replacing shadows with the diffuse color. There are two ways to enable self-illumination in 3ds Max. Either you can check the box located in this group and use a self-illumination color or use the spinner.

Note: Self-illuminated materials
Self-illuminated materials do not show shadows cast onto them. Also, they are unaffected by the lights in the scene.

Opacity Group

You can use the controls in this group, to make a material opaque, transparent, or translucent. To change the opacity of the material, change opacity to a value less than **100%**. If you want to use a map for controlling opacity, click **Opacity** map button.

Specular Highlight Group

Phong, **Blinn**, and **Oren-Nayar-Blinn** shaders produce circular highlights and share same highlight controls. **Blinn** and **Oren-Nayar-Blinn** shaders produce soft and round highlights than the **Phong** shader. You can use the **Specular Level** control to increase or decrease the strength of a highlight. As you change the value for this control, the **Highlight** curve and the highlight in the preview changes. The shape of this curve affects the blending between the specular and diffuse color components of the material. If the curve is steeper, there will be less blending and the edge of the specular highlight will be sharper. To increase or decrease the size of the highlight, change the value for **Glossiness**. **Soften** softens the specular highlights specially those formed by the glancing light.

Extended Parameters Rollout

The **Extender Parameters** rollout [see Figure 11] is same for all shaders except **Strauss** and **Translucent** shaders. The controls in this rollout allow you to control the transparency and reflection settings. Also, it has controls for adjusting the wireframe rendering.

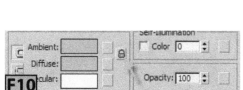
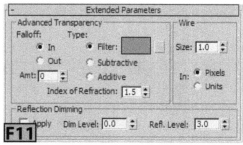

Advanced Transparency Group

These controls do not appear for the **Translucent** shader. **Falloff** allows you to set the falloff and its extent. **In** increases transparency toward the inside of the object (like glass bottle) whereas **Out** increases transparency toward the outside of the object (like clouds). **Amt** lets you adjust the amount of transparency at the outside or inside extreme.

The **Type** controls let you specify how transparency is applied. The **Filter** color swatch computes a filter color that it multiplies with the color behind the transparent surface. The **Subtractive** option subtracts from the color behind the transparent surface. The **Additive** option adds to the color behind the transparent surface.

Index of Refraction allows you to set the index of refraction used by refraction map and raytracing.

Reflection Dimming group

This group does not appear for the **Strauss** shader. These controls dim the reflection in shadow. Check **Apply** to enable reflection dimming. **Dim Level** controls the amount of dimming that takes place in shadow. **Refl. Level** affects the intensity of the reflection that is not in shadow.

SuperSampling Rollout

The **SuperSampling** rollout [see Figure 12] is used by the **Architectural, Raytrace, Standard,** and **Ink 'n Paint** materials to improve the quality of the rendered image. It performs an additional antialiasing pass on the material thus resulting in more render time. By default, a single **SuperSampling** method is applied to all materials in the scene.

Note: Super Sampling
*The **Super Sampling** method is ignored by mental ray as it has its own sampling algorithm.*

Warning: Super Sampling and Scanline Renderer
*If you turn off **Antialiasing** on the default **Scanline Renderer** rollout, **SuperSampling** settings are ignored.*

Maps Rollout

The **Maps** rollout [see Figure 13] is available for all materials. The controls in this rollout allow you to assign maps to various components of the material. To assign map to a component, click a map button. Now, choose the desired map option from the **Material/Map Browser** that opens.

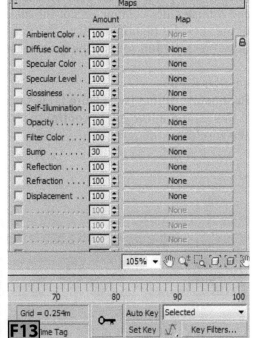

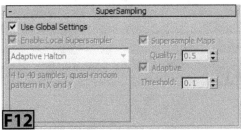

A-4 SECTION-A

Blinn Shader

This is the default shader. It produces rounder, softer highlights than the **Phong** shader. The **Blinn** and **Phong** shaders have the same basic parameters.

Metal Shader

You can use the **Metal** shader to create realistic-looking metallic surfaces and a variety of organic-looking materials. The metal material calculates their specular color automatically. The output specular color depends on the diffuse color of the material and the color of the light.

This shader produces distinctive highlights. Like the **Phong** shader, **Specular Level** still controls intensity. However, **Glossiness** affects both the intensity and size of the specular highlights. Figure 14 shows the controls in **Metal Basic Parameters** rollout.

Oren-Nayar-Blinn Shader

This shader is a variant of the **Blinn** shader and can be used to model matte surfaces such as fabric. It has two additional controls to model a surface with the matte look: **Diffuse Level** and **Roughness**.

[Oren-Nayar-Blinn Basic Parameters rollout > Advanced Diffuse Group]
Diffuse Level controls [see Figure 15] the brightness of the diffuse component of the material. It allows you to make the material lighter or darker. **Roughness** allows you to control the rate at which the diffuse component blends into the ambient component.

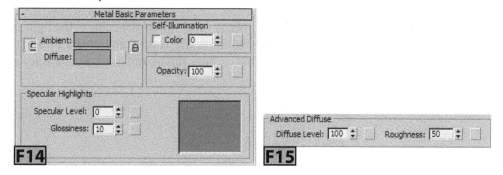

Note: The Roughnesss Parameter
The **Roughness** parameter is available only with the **Oren-Nayar-Blinn** and **Multi-Level** shaders, and with the **Arch & Design** material (mental ray).

Note: Diffuse Level control
The **Blinn**, **Metal**, **Phong**, and **Strauss** shaders do not have the **Diffuse Level** control.

Strauss Shader

This shader is a simpler version of the **Metal** shader. It can be used to model the metallic surfaces.

Strauss Basic Parameters Rollout

The Color control [see Figure 16] lets you specify the color of the material. The **Strauss** shader automatically calculates the ambient and specular color components. **Glossiness** controls the size and intensity of the specular highlights. On increasing the value for this control, the highlight gets smaller and the material appears shiner. The **Metalness** control adjust the metalness of the surface. The effect of this control is more prominent when you increase the **Glossiness** value. Opacity sets the transparency of the material.

Anisotropic Shader

You can use this shader to create surfaces with elliptical, anisotropic highlights. This shader is suitable for modeling hair, glass, or brushed metal. The **Diffuse Level** controls are similar to that of the **Oren-Nayar-Blinn** shading controls, and basic parameters controls are similar to that of the **Blinn** or **Phong** shading, except the **Specular Highlights** parameters.

The **Specular Level** [Figure 17] control sets the intensity of the specular highlights. On increasing the value for this control, the highlight goes brighter. **Glossiness** controls the size of the specular highlights. The **Anisotropy** controls the anisotropy or shape of the highlight. **Orientation** controls the orientation of the highlight. This value is measured in degrees.

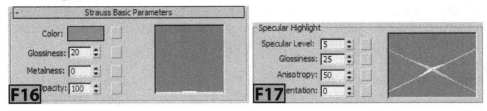

Multi-Layer Shader

This shader is similar to the **Anisotropic** shader. However, it allows you to layer two sets of specular highlights. The highlights are layered that allows you to create complex highlights. Figure 18 shows the two specular layers in the **Multi-Layer Basic Parameters** rollout.

Translucent Shader

This shader is similar to the **Blinn** shader but allows you set the translucency of the material. A translucent object not only allows light to pass through but it also scatters light within.

The **Translucent Clr** control [see Figure 19] sets the translucency color that is the color of the light scattered within the material. This color is different from the **Filter** color which is the color transmitted through transparent or semi-transparent material such as glass. The **Opacity** control sets the opacity or transparency of the material.

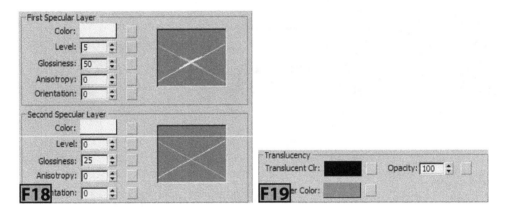

Note: The mental ray renderer
*The **mental ray** renderer is used in the examples and hands-on-exercises in this book.*

Example -1: Creating the Gold Material

Load **defMat.max** in 3ds Max. Press **M** to open the **Slate Material Editor**. On the **Material/Map Browser | Materials | Standard rollout**, drag the **Standard** material to the active view. Rename the material as **goldMat**. Apply the material to **geo1**, **geo2**, and **geo3**. Save the scene as **goldMat.max**.

On the **Parameter Editor | goldMat | Shader Basic Parameters rollout**, choose **Multi-Layer** from the drop-down. On the **Multi-Layer Basic Parameters** rollout, set **Diffuse** to **RGB(148, 70, 0)** and then set **Diffuse Level** to **25**. Take a test render [see Figure 20].

Now, we will add specularity and reflection to add the detail.

On the **First Specular Layer** section, set **Color** to **RGB (247, 227, 10)**. Set **Level** to **114**, **Glossiness** to **32**, **Anisotropy** to **82**, and **Orientation** to **90**. On the **Second Specular Layer** section, set **Color** to **RGB (192, 77, 8)**. Set **Level** to **114**, **Glossiness** to **32**, **Anisotropy** to **82**, and **Orientation** to **90**. On the **Maps** rollout, click **Reflection** map button. On the **Material Map Browser** that appears, double-click **Falloff**. On the **Parameter Editor | Falloff | Falloff Parameters rollout**, click white swatch map button. On the **Material Map Browser** that appears, double-click **Raytrace**. Set **Falloff Type** to **Fresnel**. Take a test render [see Figure 21].

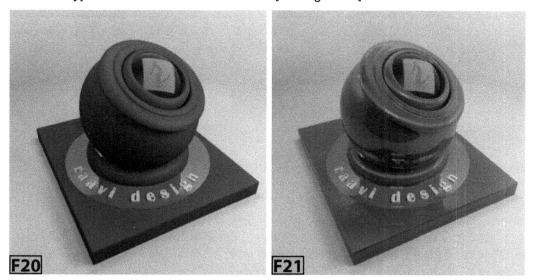

On the **Falloff | Mix Curve rollout**, RMB click on the first point and then choose **Bezier-Corner** from the contextual menu [see Figure 22]. Similarly, convert second point to **Bezier-Corner** and change the shape of the curve as shown in Figure 23. Now, take a render to view the final result [see Figure 24]. Press **Ctrl+S** to save the scene.

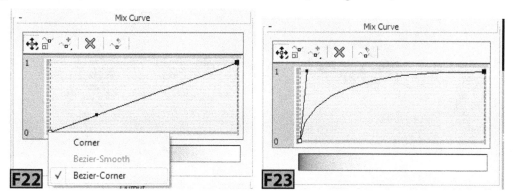

Example-2: Creating the Copper Material

Make sure the **goldMat.max** file that you created in **Example-1** is open in 3ds Max. Press **M** to open the **Slate Material Editor**, if not already open. Create a copy of the **goldMat** node by shift dragging it [see Figure 25].

Rename the node as **copperMat** and then apply it to **geo1**, **geo2**, and **geo3**. Save the scene as **copperMat.max**.

On the **Multi-Layer Basic Parameters** rollout, set **Diffuse** to **RGB(88, 28, 9)**. On the **First Specular Layer** section, set **Color** to **RGB (177, 75, 44)**.

On the **Second Specular Layer** section, set **Color** to **RGB (255, 123, 82)**. Take the render [see Figure 26] and then press **Ctrl+S** to save the file.

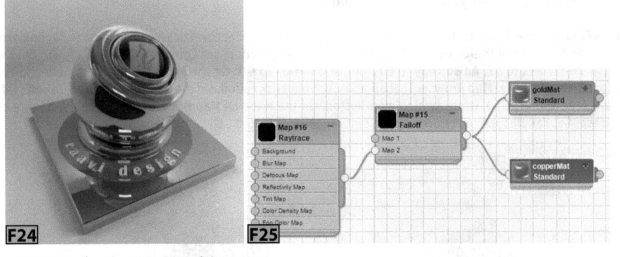

F24

F25

Example-3: Creating the Brass Material

Make sure the **copperMat.max** file that you created in Example 2 is open in 3ds Max. Press **M** to open the **Slate Material Editor**, if not already open. Create a copy of the **copperMat** node by Shift dragging it. Rename the node as **brassMat** and then apply it to **geo1, geo2,** and **geo3**. Save the scene as **brassMat.max**. On the **Multi-Layer Basic Parameters** rollout, set **Diffuse** to **RGB(49, 38, 14)**. On the **First Specular Layer** section, set **Color** to **RGB (212, 154, 30)**. On the **Second Specular Layer** section, set **Color** to **RGB (174, 98, 61)**. Take the render [see Figure 27] and then save the file with the name **brassMat.max**.

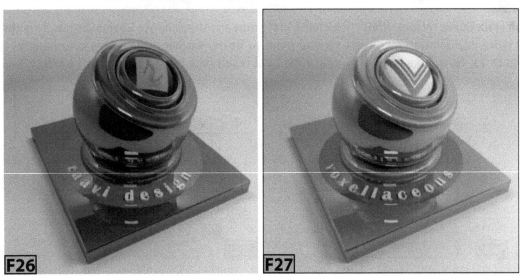

F26

F27

Example-4: Creating the Chrome Material

Load **defMat.max** in 3ds Max. Press **M** to open the **Slate Material Editor**. On the **Material/Map Browser | Materials | Standard rollout**, drag the **Standard** material to the active view. Rename the material as **chromeMat**. Apply the material to **geo1, geo2,** and **geo3**. Save the scene as **chromeMat.max**. On the **Parameter Editor | chromeMat | Blinn Basic Parameters rollout**, click the **Diffuse** color swatch. On the **Color Selector : Diffuse Color** dialog, set **Value** to **12** and click **OK**. On the **Specular Highlights** section, set **Specular Level** to **150** and **Glossiness** to **80**.

On the **Maps** rollout, set **Reflection** to **90** and then click the **Reflection** map button. On the **Material Map Browser** that appears, double-click **Raytrace**. On the **Raytrace map | Raytracer Parameters | Background section**, click **None**. On the **Material Map Browser** that appears, double-click **Bitmap**. In the **Select Bitmap Image File** dialog that appears, select **refMap.jpeg**. Render the scene [see Figure 28].

In this example, you will create the brushed aluminum material using Photoshop and 3ds Max.

Start **Photoshop**. Create a **1000 x 1000** px document and fill it with **50%** gray color. Choose **Noise | Add Noise** from the **Filter** menu and then set the parameters as shown in Figure 29 and then click **OK**.

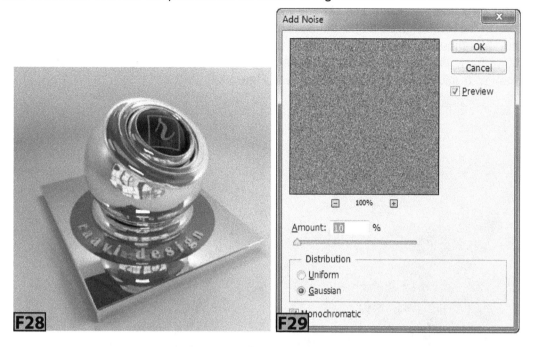

Choose **Blur | Motion Blur** from the **Filter** menu and then set the parameters as shown in Figure 30 and then click **OK**. Choose **Adjustments | Brightness\Contrast** from the **Image** menu and then set the parameters as shown in Figure 31 and then click **OK**. Save the document as **scratch.jpg**.

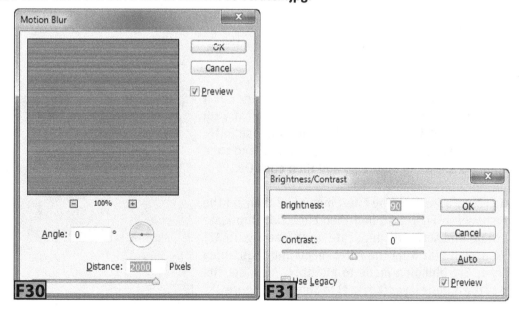

Load **defMat.max** in 3ds Max. Press **M** to open the **Slate Material Editor**. On the **Material/Map Browser | Materials | Standard rollout**, drag the **Standard** material to the active view. Rename the material as **balMat**. Apply the material to **geo1, geo2,** and **geo3**.

Save the scene as **balMat.max**.

On the **Parameter Editor | balMat | Shader Basic Parameters rollout**, choose **Oren-Nayar-Blinn** from the drop-down. On the **Parameter Editor | balMat | Oren-Nayar-Blinn Basic Parameters rollout**, click **Ambient** color swatch. On the **Color Selector : Ambient Color** dialog, set **Value** to **84** and click **OK**. Unlock the **Ambient** and **Diffuse** components of the material.

Click the **Diffuse** map button and then on the **Material Map Browser** that appears, double-click **Mix**. On the **Parameter Editor | Mix map**, set **Color 1** to **127** and assign **scratch.jpg** to **Color 2** using the **Bitmap** map. Set **Mix Amount** to **72%**. On the **balMat | Oren-Nayar-Blinn Basic Parameters rollout | Advanced Diffuse section**, set **Diffuse Level** to **81**, and **Roughness** to **80**. Now, take a test render [see Figure 32]. On the **Parameter Editor | balMat | Oren-Nayar-Blinn Basic Parameters rollout | Specular Highlight section**, set **Specular Level** to **156**, **Glossiness** to **13**, and **Soften** to **0.48**. Now, take a test render [see Figure 33].

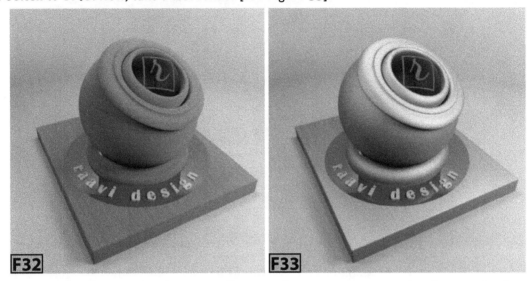

On the **Parameter Editor | scratch.jpg | Output rollout**, set **Output Amount** to **0.6**. Take a render [see Figure 34]. Press **Ctrl+S** to save the file.

Example-6: Creating the Denim Fabric Material

In this example, you will create the denim fabric material using **Photoshop** and **3ds Max**.

Start Photoshop. Create a **1000 x 1000** px document and fill it with **RGB (41, 67, 102)** color. Create a new layer and fill it with **50%** gray. Press **D** to switch to the default colors. Choose **Filter Gallery| Sketch | Halftone Pattern** from the **Filter** menu and then set the parameters as shown in Figure 35 and then click **OK**.

Choose **Pixelate | Mezzotint** from the **Filter** menu and then set the parameters as shown in Figure 36 and then click **OK**. Duplicate the layer and rotate and scale the duplicate layer [see Figure 37]. Choose **Blur | Gaussian Blur** from the **Filter** menu and then apply a blur of radius **1**. Set blending mode to **Multiply**. Also, set the blending mode of the middle layer (**Layer 1**) to **Softlight** [Figure 38].

Save the file as **denimFebric.jpg**. Choose **Flatten Image** from the **Layer** menu to flatten the image. Now, press **Ctrl+Shift+U** to desaturate the image and then save it as **denimFebricBump.jpg**. Load **defMat.max** in 3ds Max. Press **M** to open the **Slate Material Editor**. On the **Material/ Map Browser | Materials | Standard rollout**, drag the **Standard** material to the active view. Rename the material as **denimMat**. Apply the material to **geo1**, **geo2**, and **geo3**.

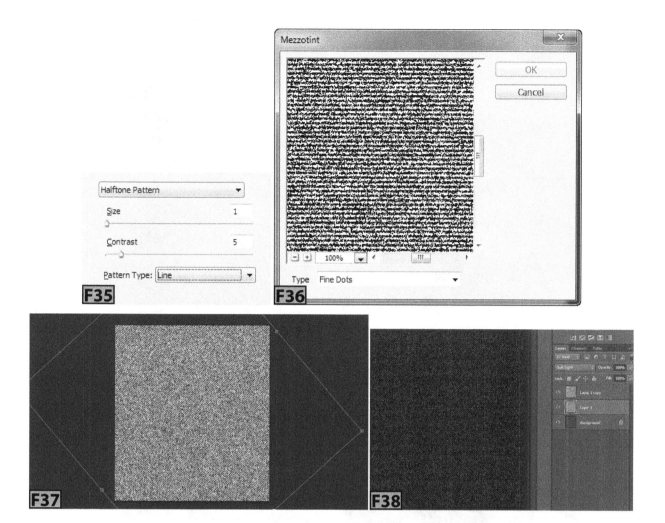

Save the scene as **denimMat.max**. On the **Parameter Editor | denimMat | Shader Basic Parameters rollout**, choose **Oren-Nayar-Blinn** from the drop-down. On the **Parameter Editor | denimMat | Oren-Nayar-Blinn Basic Parameters rollout**, click **Ambient** color swatch. On the **Color Selector : Ambient Color** dialog, set **RGB** to **50, 53, 57** and click **OK**. Unlock the **Ambient** and **Diffuse** components of the material. Click the **Diffuse** map button and then on the **Material Map Browser** that appears, double-click **Bitmap**. Assign **denimFebric.jpg**.

On the **denimMat | Oren-Nayar-Blinn Basic Parameters rollout | Advanced Diffuse section**, set **Diffuse Level** to **250**, and **Roughness** to **75**. Now, take a test render [see Figure 39]. On the **Parameter Editor | denimMat | Oren-Nayar-Blinn Basic Parameters rollout | Specular Highlight section**, set **Specular Level** to **7**, and **Glossiness** to **10**. Take a test render [see Figure 40]. On the **Maps** rollout, ensure **Bump** is set to **30%** and then click **Bump** map button. On the **Material Map Browser** that appears, double-click **Bitmap**. On the **Select Bitmap Image File** dialog that appears, select **denimFebricBump.jpg**. Take a test render [see Figure 41]. Press **Ctrl+S** to save the file.

Compound Materials

Compound materials are used to combine two or more sub-materials. These materials are especially useful when you use map mask with them.

Blend Material

The **Blend** material allows you to mix two materials on a single side of the surface. You can use the **Mix Amount** parameter [see Figure 42] to control the way two materials are blended together. You can also animate this control. The **Material 1** and **Material 2** controls let you assign the two materials to be blended. You can also use the corresponding check boxes to turn material on or off. The **Interactive** option specifies which of the materials or mask map will be displayed in the viewport by the interactive renderer.

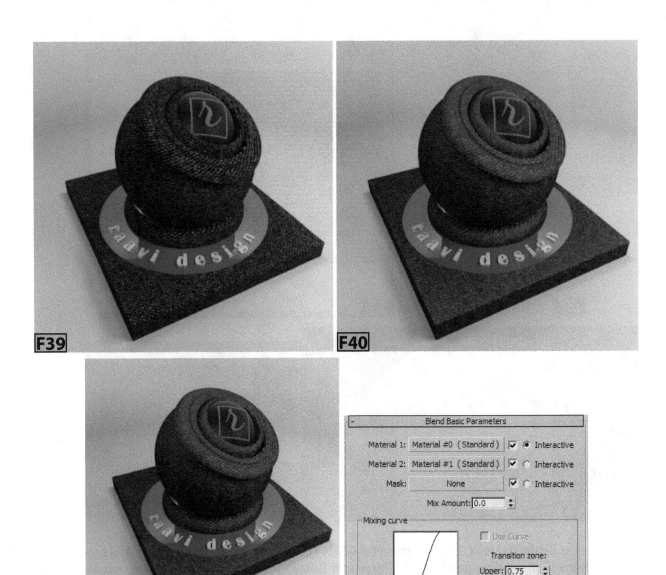

The **Mask** control lets you assign a map as mask. The lighter and darker areas on the mask map control the degree of blending. The lighter areas displays more of the **Material 1** whereas the darker areas show more of **Material 2**. The **Mix** Amount controls the proportion of blend in degrees. A value of **0** means only **Material 1** will be visible on the surface whereas a value of **100** means **Material 2** will be visible on the surface.

When you assign a mask map for blending, you can use the mixing curve to affect the blending. You can use the controls in the **Transition Zone** group to adjust the level of the **Upper** and **Lower** limits.

Note: Interactive renderer and Blend material
Only one map can be displayed in the viewports when using the interactive renderer.

Note: Blend Material and Noise Map
*The **Mix Amount** control is not available when you use mask to blend the material. Using a **Noise** map as mixing map can produce naturally looking surfaces.*

Load **defMat.max** in 3ds Max. Save the scene as **blendMat.max**. Press **M** to open the **Slate Material Editor**. On the **Material/Map Browser | Materials | Standard rollout**, drag the **Blend** material to the active view. Rename the materials connected to the **Blend** node as **mat1** and **mat2**. Apply the **Blend** material to **geo1, geo2,** and **geo3**.

Assign **ConcreteBare.jpg** to the **mat1 | Diffuse** map and **ConcreteBare1.jpg** to the **mat2 | Diffuse** map. Take a test render [see Figure 43]. Assign a **Noise** map to the **Blend** material's **Mask** control. On the **Mixing Curve** section, check the **Use Curve** check box and set **Upper** to **0.78** and **Lower** to **0.3**. Take a test render [see Figure 44].

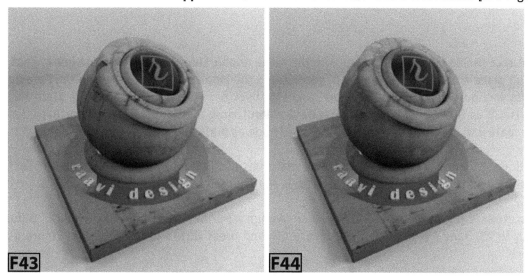

F43   F44

On the **Parameter Editor | Noise Parameters rollout**, set **Noise Type** to **Fractal**, **High** to **0.9**, and **Size** to **15.5**. Take a test render and press **Ctrl+S** to save the file. For the sake of clarity, I have rendered [see Figure 45] a plane with **mat1** (left image), **mat2** (middle image), and **Blend** (right image) materials applied. Figure 46 shows the node network.

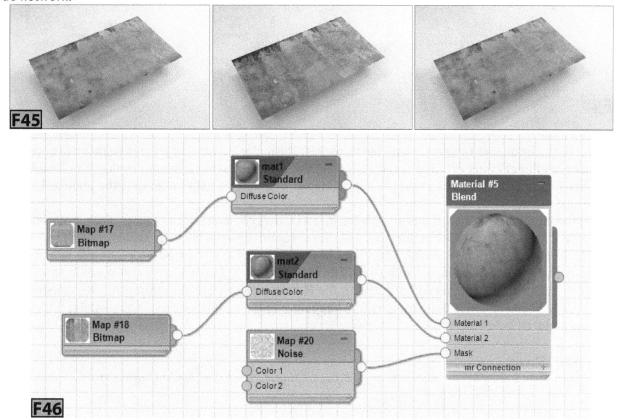

F45

F46

Double Sided Material

The **Double Sided** material lets you assign two different materials to the front and back surface of an object. The **Facing Material** and **Back Material** controls [see Figure 47] allow you to specify the material for the front and back faces, respectively. The **Translucency** control allows you to blend the two materials. There will be no blending of the materials if **Translucency** is set to **0**. At a value of **100**, the outer material will be visible on the inner faces and inner material will be visible on the outer faces.

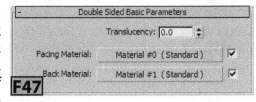

F47

Example-8: Working with the Double Sided Material

Load **defMat.max** in 3ds Max. Save the file with the name **doubleSidedMat.max**. Delete **geo4, geo1, geo6** from the scene and place a teapot at the center of **geo5**. Go to the **Modify** panel and then on the **Parameters rollout | Teapot Parts section**, uncheck **Handle, Spout**, and **Lid** check boxes. Press **M** to open the **Slate Material Editor**. On the **Material/Map Browser | Materials | Standard rollout**, drag the **Double Sided** material to the active view. Rename the materials connected to the **DoubleSided** node as **mat1** and **mat2**. Apply the material to the teapot.

Now, we will assign maps to the back and facing materials of the **Double Sided** material. The **Facing Material** is represented by **mat1** whereas the **Back Material** is represented by **mat2**.

Assign **ConcreteBare.jpg** to the **mat1 | Diffuse** map. Assign a **Perlin Marble** map to the **mat2 | Diffuse** map. Set **Translucency** to **25**. Take a test render [see Figure 48] and press **Ctrl+S** to save the file. Figure 49 shows the node network.

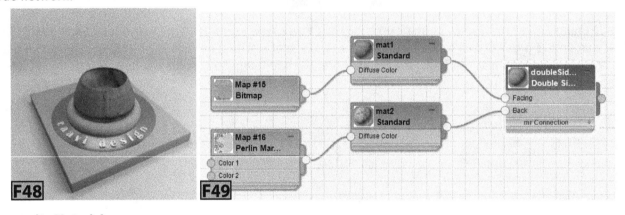

F48   **F49**

Composite Material

This material can be used to composite upto ten materials. The materials are composited from top to bottom. The maps can be combined using additive opacity, subtractive opacity, or using an amount value. The **Base Material** control [see Figure 50] allows you to set the base material. The default base material is the **Standard** material.

The **Mat.1** to **Mat.9** controls are used to specify the material that you want to composite. Each material control has an array of buttons called **ASM** buttons. These buttons control how the material is composited. The **A** button allows you to use the additive opacity. The colors in the materials are summed based on the opacity. The **S** button allows you to use the subtractive opacity. The **M** button is used to mix the materials using a value. You can enter the value in the spinner located next to the **M** button. When the **M** button is active, amount ranges from **0** to **100**. When amount is **0**, no compositing happens and the material below is not visible. If the amount is **100**, the material below is visible.

Tip: Composite Material v Composite Map
If you want to achieve a result by combings maps instead of combining materials, use the **Composite** *map that provides greater control.*

Note: Overloaded compositing

*For additive and subtractive compositing, the amount can range from **0** to **200**. When the amount is greater than **100**, the compositing is overloaded. As a result, the transparent area of the material becomes more opaque.*

Morpher Material

The **Morpher** material is used with the **Morpher** modifier. For example, when a character raises his eyebrows, you can use this material to display wrinkles on his forehead. You can blend the materials the same way you morph the geometry using the channel spinners of the **Morpher** modifier.

Multi/Sub-Object Material

The **Multi/Sub-Object** material allows you to assign materials at the sub-object level. The number field [see Figure 51] shows the number of sub-materials contained in the **Multi/Sub-Object** material. You can use the **Set Number** button to set the number of sub-materials that make up the material. The **Add** button allows you to a new sub-material to the list. Use the **Delete** button to remove currently chosen sub-material from the list. The **ID**, **Name**, and **Sub-Material** controls allow you to sort the list based on the material id, name, and sub-material, respectively.

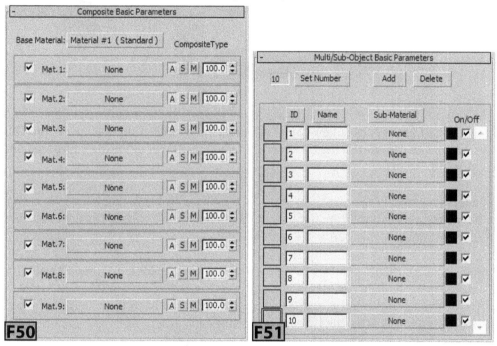

To assign materials to the sub-objects, select the object and assign the **Multi/sub-Object** material to it. Apply a **Mesh Select** modifier to the object. Activate the **Face** sub-object level. Now, select the faces to which you will assign the material. Apply a **Material Modifier** and then set the material ID value to the number of the sub-material you need to assign.

Shellac Material

Shellac material allows you to mix two materials by superimposing one over the other. The superimposed material is known as the **Shellac** material. The **Base Material** control [Figure 52] lets you choose or edit the base sub-material. The **Shellac Material** control lets you choose or edit the **Shellac** material. The **Shellac Color Blend** control adjusts the amount of color mixing. The default value for this control is **0**. Hence, the shellac material has no effect on the surface. There is no upper limit for this control. Higher values overload the colors of the **Shellac** material. You can also animate this parameter.

Example-9: Working with the Shellac Material

Ensure that **doubleSidedMat.max** is open in 3ds Max. Press **M** to open the **Slate Material Editor**. On the **Material/ Map Browser | Materials | Standard rollout**, drag the **Shellac** material to the active view. Rename the materials connected to the **Base Material** and **Shellac Mat** ports of the **Shellac** node as **mat1** and **mat2**, respectively. Apply the material to the teapot.

Assign the **Swirl** map to the **mat1 | Diffuse** map and **Wood** map to the **mat2 | Diffuse** map. Set **Shellac Color Blend** to **86**. Take a test render [see Figure 53].

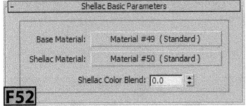

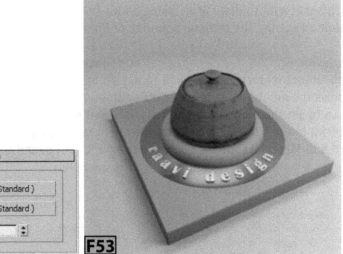

Top/Bottom Material

This material lets you assign two different materials to the top and bottom portions of an object. You can also blend the two materials. The top faces of an object are those faces whose normals point up. The bottom faces have the normals down. You can control the boundary between the top and bottom using the controls available in the **Coordinates** group [see Figure 54].

The **World** option lets you specify the direction according to the world coordinates of the scene. If you rotate the object, the boundary between the top and bottom faces remains in place. The **Local** option allows you to control the direction using the local coordinate system.

You can specify the top and bottom materials using the **Top** and **Bottom** controls, respectively. The **Swap** button allows you to swap the material. You can blend the edge between the top and bottom materials using the **Blend** control. The value for this control ranges from **0** to **1**. If you set **Blend** to **0**, there will be a sharp line between the top and bottom materials. At **100**, the two materials tint each other.

The **Position** control allows you to specify the location where the division between the two materials will occur. The value for this control ranges from **0** to **1**. If you set **Position** to **0**, only top material will be displayed. At **100**, only bottom material will be displayed.

Raytrace Material

This material is an advanced surface-shading material. It supports the same diffuse surface shading that a **Standard** material supports. However, it also supports fog, color density, translucency, fluorescence, and other special effects. This material is capable of creating fully raytraced reflections and refractions. Figure 55 shows the **Raytrace** material's interface.

Matte/Shadow Material

The **Matte Shadow** material is used to make whole objects or any set of faces into matte objects. The matte objects revel the background color or the environment map. A matte object is invisible but it blocks any geometry behind it however it does not block the background. The matte objects can also receive shadows. The shadows cast on the matte object are applied to the alpha channel. To properly generate shadows on a matte object, turn off **Opaque Alpha** and then turn on **Affect Alpha** [see Figure 56].

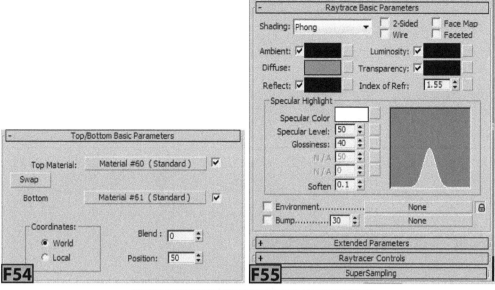

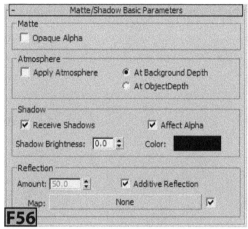

Ink 'n Paint Material

The **Ink 'n Paint** material is used to create cartoons effects. This material produces shading with inked borders.

The Last Word

In this section, you have learned about the standard and other related materials. You have also used standard maps such as **Bitmap, Falloff, Raytrace,** and so forth. 3ds Max provides many other maps that you can use to enhance the look of the materials. In the next section, you will learn about various standard maps available in 3ds Max.

B-Standard Maps

Maps allow you to improve the appearance of the materials. They also help you to enhance the realism of the materials. You can use maps in a variety of ways, you can use them to create environments, to create image planes for modeling, to create projections from light, and so forth. You can use the **Material/Map Browser** to load a map or create a map of a particular type. A map can be used to design different elements of a material such as reflection, refraction, bump, and so forth.

Maps and Mapping Coordinates

When you apply a map to any object, the object must have mapping coordinates applied. These coordinates are specified in terms of UVW axes local to the object. Most of the objects in 3ds Max have the **Generate Mapping Coordinates** option. When on, 3ds Max generates default mapping coordinates.

UVW Mapping Coordinate Channels

Each object in 3ds Max can have **99** UVW mapping coordinates. The default mapping is always assigned the number **1**. The **UVW Map** modifier can send coordinates to any of these 99 channels.

3ds Max gives you ability to generate the mapping coordinates in different ways:

- The **Generate Mapping Coords** option is available for most of the primitives. This option provides a projection appropriate to the shape of the object type.
- Apply the **Unwrap UVW** modifier. This modifier comes with some useful tools that you can use to edit mapping coordinates.
- Apply the **UVW Map** modifier. This modifier allows you to set a projection type from several projection types it provides.

Here's the quick rundown to the projection types:

- **Box projection:** It places a duplicate of the map image on each of the six sides of a box.

- **Cylindrical projection:** This wraps the image around the sides of the object. The duplicate images are also projected onto the end caps.

- **Spherical projection:** This projection type wraps the map image around a sphere and gather the image at the top and bottom.

- **Shrink-wrap projection:** This type is like the spherical projection but creates one singularity instead of two.

- Use special mapping coordinates. For example, the **Loft** object provides built-in mapping coordinates.
- Use a **Surface Mapper** modifier. This modifier uses a map assigned to a NURBS surface and projects it onto the object(s).

Here's quick rundown to the cases when you can apply a map and you don't need mapping coordinates:

- **Reflection**, **Refraction**, and **Environment** maps.
- 3D Procedural maps: **Noise** and **Marble**.
- **Face-mapped** materials.

Real-World Mapping

The real-world mapping is an alternative mapping method that you can use in 3ds Max. This type of mapping considers the correct scaling of the texture mapped materials applied to the geometry in the scene.

Note: Autodesk Materials
Autodesk Materials require you to use the real-world mapping.

In order to apply the real-world mapping correctly, two requirements must be met. First, the correct style of UV texture coordinates must be assigned to the geometry. In other words, the size of the UV space should correspond to the size of the geometry. To address this issue, the **Real-World Map Size** check box is added to the many rollouts in 3ds Max [see Figure 1].

The second requirement is available in the **Coordinates** rollout of the **Material Editor. Use Real-World Scale** is on in 3ds Max Design [see Figure 2] whereas in 3ds Max it is off [see Figure 3]. When this check box is off, **U/V** changes to **Width/Height** and **Tiling** changes to **Size**.

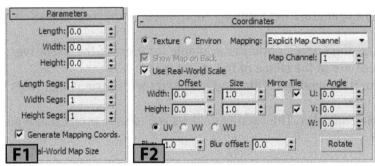

Note: Real-world Mapping
The real-world mapping is off in 3ds Max, by default. However, in 3ds Max Design its on.

Tip: Real-World Map Size check box
You can turn on **Real-World Map Size** *by default from the* **Preferences** *dialog by using the* **Use Real-World Texture Coordinates** *check box. This option is available in the* **Texture Coordinates** *section of the* **General** *panel.*

Output Rollout

The options in this rollout [see Figure 4] are responsible for setting the internal parameters of a map. These options can be used to determine the rendered appearance of the map. Most of the controls on this rollout are for the color output.

Note: Output Rollout
These controls do not affect the bump maps except the **Invert** *toggle, which reverses the direction of the bumps and bump amount.*

2D Maps

The 2D maps are two-dimensional images that are mapped to the surface of the geometric objects. You can also use them to create environment maps. The **Bitmap** is the simplest type 2D maps. 3ds Max also allows you to create 2D maps procedurally.

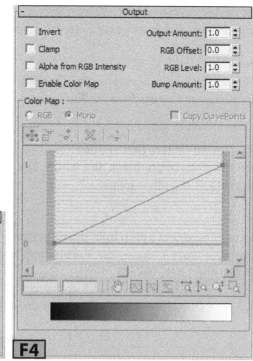

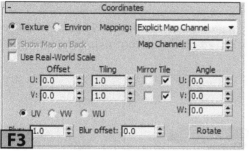

Coordinates Rollout

The **Coordinates** rollout shown in Figures 2 and 3 allows you to adjust coordinate parameters to move a map relative to the surface of the object. This rollout also allows you to set tiling and mirroring of the texture pattern. The repetition of the texture pattern on the surface of an object is known as tiling. The mirroring is a form of tiling in which 3ds Max repeats the map and then flips the repeated map.

In this rollout, there are two options that you can use to control the mapping type. These options are **Texture** and **Environ**. The **Texture** type applies texture as a map to the surface. The **Environ** type uses map as an environment map. For both of these options, you can select the types of coordinates from the **Mapping** drop-down.

Here's the list of options available in the **Mapping** drop-down:

- **Explicit Map Channel:** It uses any map channel from **1** to **99**. When you select this option, **Map Channel** becomes active.
- **Vertex Color Channel:** This option uses assigned vertex colors as a channel.
- **Planar from Object XYZ:** This option uses planar mapping based on the object's local coordinates.
- **Planar from World XYZ:** This option uses planar mapping based on the scene's world coordinates.
- **Spherical Environment/Cylindrical Environment/Shrink-wrap Environment:** These options project the map into the scene as if it were mapped to an invisible object in the background.
- **Screen:** This option projects a map as a flat backdrop in the scene.

Noise Rollout

You can add a random noise to the appearance of the material using the parameters available in this rollout [see Figure 5]. These parameters modify the mapping of pixels by applying a fractal noise function.

Bitmap

This map is the simplest type of map available in 3ds Max. This map is useful for creating many type of materials from wood to skin. If you want to create an animated material, you can use an animation or video file with this map. When you select this map, the **Select Bitmap Image File** dialog opens. Navigate to the location where the bitmap file is stored and then click **Open** to select the file.

Checker Map

This map is a procedural texture that applies a two-color checkerboard pattern [see Figure 6]. The default colors used to produce the pattern are black and white. You can also change these colors with map and it's true for all color components of the other maps.

Camera Map Per Pixel Map

This map allows you to project a map from the direction of a particular camera. It is useful when you are working on a matte painting. Figure 7 shows the **Marble** map projected on the teapot using the camera [see Figure 8]. Figure 9 shows the node network.

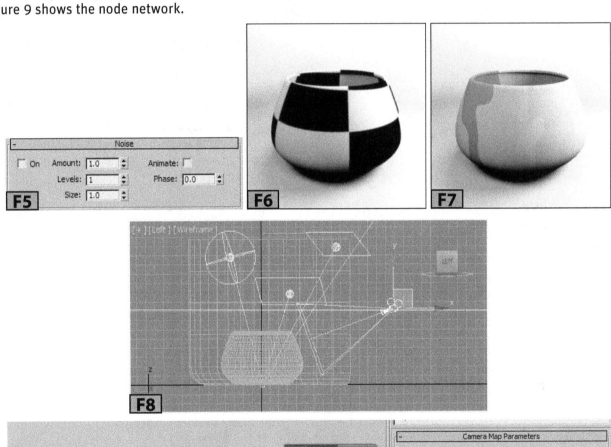

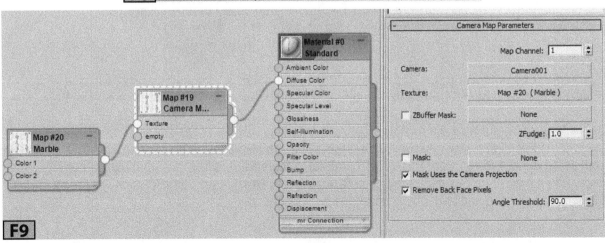

Gradient Map

This map type allows you to create a gradient that shades from one color to another. Figure 10 shows the shift from one color to another. The red, green, and blue colors are used for the gradient. Figure 11 shows the result when the fractal noise is applied to the gradient. Figure 12 shows the node network.

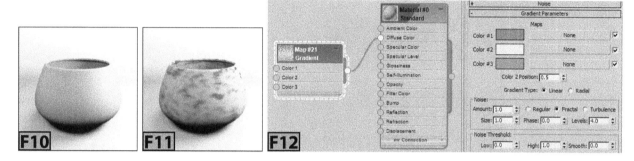

Gradient Ramp Map

This map is similar to the **Gradient** map. Like the **Gradient** map, it shades from one color to another, however, you can use any number of colors [see Figure 13]. Also, you have additional controls to create a complex customized ramp. Figure 14 shows the node network used to produce the result shown in Figure 13.

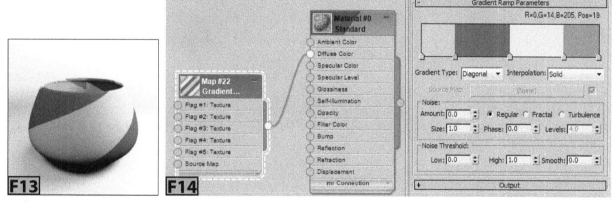

Normal Bump Map

This map allows you to connect a texture-baked normal map to a material. Figure 15 shows the bump on the surface created using the **Normal Bump** map. Figure 16 shows the node network.

Substance Map

This map is used with the **Substance** parametric textures. These textures are resolution-independent 2D textures and use less memory. Therefore, they are useful for exporting to the game engines via the **Algorithmic Substance Air** middleware.

Swirl Map

This map is 2D procedural map that can be used to simulate swirls [see Figure 17].

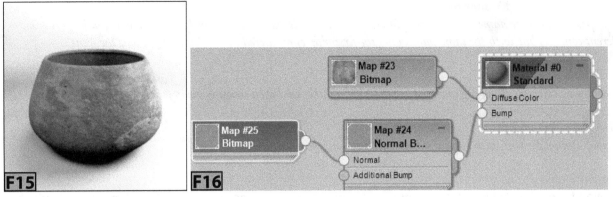

F15   F16

Tile Map

You can use this map to create a brick or stacked tiling of colors or maps. A number of commonly used architectural brick patterns are available with this map. Figure 18 shows render with the **English Bond** type applied.

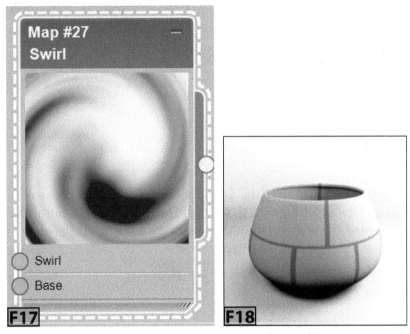

F17   F18

Vector Map

Using this map, you can apply a vector-based graphics, including animation as textures. You can also use AutoCAD Pattern (PAT) files, Adobe Illustrator (AI) files, Portable Document (PDF) files, and Scalable Vector Graphics (SVG) files.

Vector Displacement Map

This map allows you to displace the meshes in three directions whereas the traditional method permits displacement only along the surface normals.

3D Maps

3D maps are patterns generated by 3ds Max in 3D space. Let's have a look at various 3D maps.

Cellular Map

You can use this map to generate a variety of visual effects such as mosaic tiling, pebbled surfaces, and even ocean surfaces [see Figure 19].

Dent Map

This map generated a procedural map using a fractal noise algorithm [see Figure 20]. The effect that this produces depends on the map type chosen.

Falloff Map

The **Falloff** map generates a value from white to black based on the angular falloff of the face normals. Figure 21 shows the **Falloff** map applied to the geometry with the **Falloff** type set to **Fresnel**.

Marble Map

You can use this map to create a marble texture with the colored veins against [see Figure 22] a color background.

Noise Map

This map allows to create a noise map that creates the random perturbation of a surface based on the interaction of two colors or materials. Figure 23 shows the **Noise** map with the **Noise Type** set to **Fractal**.

Particle Age Map

This map is used with the particle systems. This map changes the color of the particles based on their age.

Particle MBlur Map

This map can be used to alter the opacity of the leading and trailing ends of particles based on their rate of motion.

Perlin Marble Map

This map is like the **Marble** map. However, it generates a marble pattern using the **Perlin Turbulence** algorithm.

Smoke Map

You can use this map [see Figure 24] to create animated opacity maps to simulate the effects of smoke in a beam of light, or other cloudy, flowing effects.

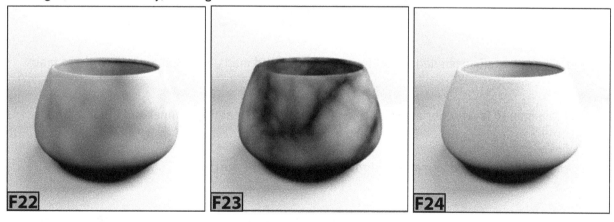

Speckle Map

This map [see Figure 25] can be used to create granite-like and other patterned surfaces.

Splat Map

This map can be used to create patterns similar to the spattered paint [see Figure 26].

Stucco Map

You can use this map [see Figure 27] as a bump to create the effect like a stuccoed surface.

Waves Map

You can use this map as both bump or diffuse map [see Figure 28]. This map is used to create watery or wavy effects.

Wood Map

This map creates a wavy grain like wood pattern [see Figure 29]. You can control the direction, thickness, and complexity of the grain.

Compositor Maps

These maps are specifically designed for compositing colors and maps. Let's have a look at these maps.

Composite Map

You can use this map to layer other maps atop each other using the alpha channel and other methods.

Mask Map

This map can be used to view one material through another on the surface.

Mix Map

With this map, you can combine two colors or materials on a single side of the surface. You can also animate the **Mix Amount** parameter to control how two maps are blended together over time.

RGB Multiply Map

This map combines two maps by multiplying their RGB values. This map is generally used as a **Bump** map.

Color Modifiers Maps
These maps change the color of the pixels in a material. Let's have a look:

Color Correction Map
This map is allows you to modify color of a map using various tools. This map uses a stack-based method.

Output Map
You can use this map to apply output settings to the procedural maps such as **Checker** or **Marble**. These maps don't have the output settings.

RGB Tint Map
This map adjusts the three color channels in an image.

Vertex Color Map
In 3ds Max, you can assign vertex colors using the **VertexPaint** modifier, the **Assign Vertex Colors** utility, or the vertex controls for an editable mesh, editable patch, or editable poly. This map makes any vertex coloring applied to an object available for rendering.

Reflection and Refraction Maps
These maps are used to create reflections and refractions. Here's is a quick rundown.

Flat Mirror Map
This map produces a material that reflects surroundings when it is applied to the co-planer faces. It is assigned to the **Reflection** map of the material.

Raytrace Map
This map allows you to create fully raytraced reflections and refractions. The reflections/refractions generated by this map are more accurate than the **Reflect/Refract** map.

Reflect/Refract Map
You can use this map to create a reflective or refractive surface. To create reflection, assign this map type to the reflection map. To create refraction, apply it to the **Refraction** map.

Thin Wall Refraction Map
This map can be used to simulate a surface as if it part of a surface through a plate of glass.

The Last Word
In this section, you have learned about various standard maps available in 3ds Max. In next section, you will use these maps to create the shading networks.

B-10 SECTION-B

C-Hands-on Exercises

In this section, you work on some hands-on exercises to understand the concepts learned in the previous two sections.

Exercises

Complete the following exercises.

HOI-1: Creating the Microscopic Material

For our first hands-on exercise, we're going to create a microscopic material [see Figure 1].

The summary of tasks you need to complete in this hands-on exercise is as follows:

F1

- Open the start file.
- Apply a Falloff map to the Diffuse component of the material.
- Mix two Noise maps using the Mix map to create the bump material.

The following material(s) and map(s) are used in this exercise: **Standard, Mix, Falloff,** and **Noise.**

Start 3ds Max. Open **hoe1_begin.max**. Press **M** to open the **Slate Material Editor** and then create a new **Standard** material and assign it to the **sphGeo** in the scene. Rename the material as **msMat.** Connect a **Falloff** map to the **msMat's** Diffuse port. On the **Parameter Editor | Falloff map | Falloff Parameters rollout | Front:Side section,** set first color swatch to **RGB (20, 20, 20)** and second color swatch to white. Set **Falloff Type** to **Perpendicular/ Parallel.** Ensure **Falloff Direction** is set to **Viewing Direction (Camera Z-Axis)** [see Figure 2]. Also, set the **Mix Curve** to as shown in Figure 3.

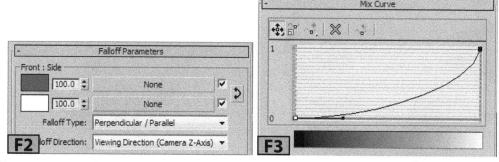

F2   F3

Now, you will create two **Noise** maps and mix them using the **Mix** map.

Connect a **Mix** map to the **msMat's** Bump port. On the **Parameter Editor | Mix map | Mix Parameters rollout,** set **Mix Amount** to **37.8.** On the **Slate Material Editor,** connect two **Noise** maps, one each to the **Color 1** and **Color 2** ports. For the **Color 1 | Noise** map use the settings shown in Figure 4. Figure 5 shows the **Noise** map settings connected to **Color 2.** Fig. 6 shows the node network.

Now, render the scene. Notice that the output is little bit on the darker side. To address this, on the **Parameter Editor | Falloff map | Falloff Parameters rollout | Front:Side section,** set first color swatch to **RGB (80, 80, 80).**

Render the scene [see Figure 1] and then save the scene with the name **hoe1.max.**

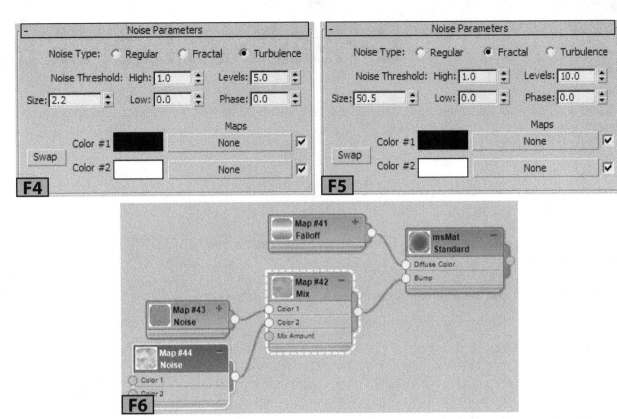

F4

F5

F6

HOI-2: Creating Material for a Volleyball

Here, we are going to apply texture to a volleyball [see Figure 7]. Left image in Figure 7 shows the reference whereas the right image shows the rendered output.

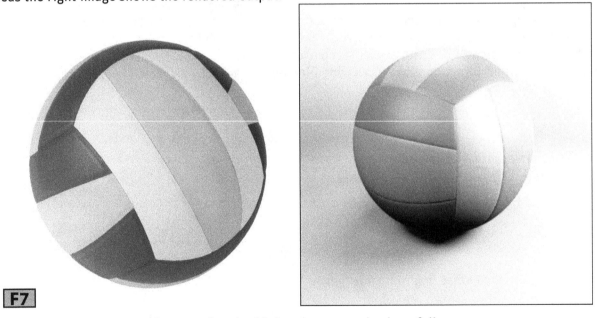

F7

The summary of tasks you need to complete in this hands-on exercise is as follows:

- Open the start file.
- Create a **Multi/Sub-Object** material and set number of materials to **3**.
- Connect three **Standard** materials to the **Multi/Sub-Object** material representing three colors of the volleyball.
- Assign **Noise** maps to create bump on the surface of the volleyball.

The following material(s) and map(s) are used in this exercise: **Multi/Sub-Object**, **Standard**, and **Noise**.

Start 3ds Max. Open **hoe2_begin.max**. Select the **VolleyBallGeo** in any viewport and then go to the **Modify** panel. On the **Selection** rollout, click **Element** and then select the elements that make the yellow part of the volleyball [see Figure 8]. See left image in Fig. 7 for reference. On the **Modify panel | Polygon: Material IDs rollout**, set set **ID** to **1** [see Figure 9]. Similarly, select the blue and white elements and assign them ID **2** and **3**, respectively.

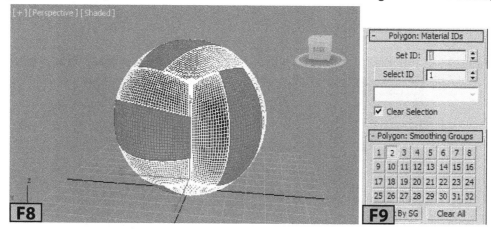

Press **M** to open the **Slate Material Editor** and then create a new **Multi/Sub-object** material and assign it to the **VolleyBallGeo** in the scene. Rename the material as **vbMat**. On the **Parameter Editor | vbMat | Multi/Sub-Object Parameters rollout**, click **Set Number** and then set **Number of Materials** to **3** in the dialog that appears. Next, click **OK**. In the **Slate Material Editor**, connect a **Standard** material to the port **1** of the **vbMat**. On the **Parameter Editor | Blinn Basic Parameter rollout**, set the **Diffuse** component to **RGB (242, 140, 8)**. On the **Specular Highlights** section, set **Specular Level** to **71** and **Glossiness** to **28**.

Connect a **Noise** map to the **Bump** port of the **Standard** material. Set **Bump** to **2%**. On the **Parameter Editor | Noise map | Noise Parameters rollout**, set **Noise Type** to **Turbulence**, **Levels** to **9**, and **Size** to **0.5**. On the **Slate Material Editor**, select the **Standard** material and **Noise** map. Now, create a copy of the selected nodes using SHIFT. Connect the new **Standard** material to the port **2** of the **vbMat**. Similarly, create another copy and connect it to port **3**. Figure 10 shows the node network.

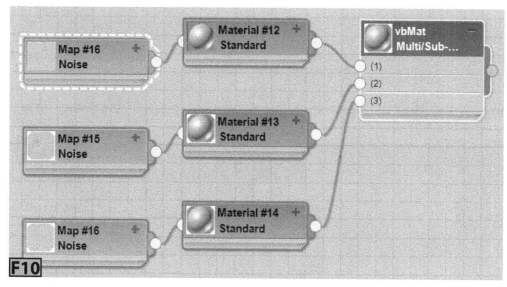

Set **Diffuse** components of the material connected to the port **2** and **3** to **RGB (11, 91, 229)** and **RGB (236, 236, 230)**, respectively. Now, press **F9** to take a render. Save the scene with the name **hoe2.max**.

Here, we are going to apply texture to a water tunnel [see Figure 11].

The summary of tasks you need to complete in this hands-on exercise is as follows:

- Open the start file.
- Create the water shader.
- Create **Diffuse** and **Displacement** textures.

The following material(s) and map(s) are used in this exercise: **Raytrace, Standard, Mix,** and **Noise.**

F11

Start 3ds Max. Open **hoe3_begin.max**. Press **M** to open the **Slate Material Editor** and then create a new **Raytrace** material and assign it to the **waterGeo** in the scene. Rename the material as **waterMat**. On the **Parameter Editor | Raytrace Basic Parameter rollout**, set **Diffuse** to black. Set **Transparency** to **RGB (146, 175, 223)**. Set **Reflect** to **RGB (178, 178, 178)**.

On the **Specular Highlight** section, set **Specular Level** to **161** and **Glossiness** to **29**. Connect a **Noise** map to the **Bump** port of the **waterMat**. Use the default values for the **Noise** map. Press **F9** to render the scene [Figure 12]. On the **Slate Material Editor**, create a new **Standard** material and assign it to the **caveGeo** in the scene. Rename the material as **caveMat**. Connect a **Mix** map to the **Diffuse** port of the **caveMat**.

Connect a **Noise** map to the **Color 1** port of the **Mix** map. On the **Noise Parameters** rollout, set **Noise Type** to **Turbulence, Levels** to **10, Size** to **31.7**. Set **Color 1** to **RGB (132, 77, 6)** and **Color 2** to **RGB (154, 100, 79)**. Connect a **Noise** map to the **Color 2** port of the **Mix** map. On the **Noise Parameters** rollout, set **Noise Type** to **Turbulence, Levels** to **10, Size** to **72**. Set **Color 1** to **RGB (212, 84, 45)** and **Color 2** to **RGB (181, 99, 54)**.

On the **Parameter Editor | Mix Parameters rollout**, set **Mix Amount** to **40**. On the **Mixing curve** section, check the **Use Curve** check box and then set **Upper** to **0.6** and **Lower** to **0.53**. Take a test render [Figure 13].

F12

F13

Connect a **Mix** map to the **Displacement** port of the **caveMat**. Set **Displacement** to **25%**. Connect a **Noise** map to the **Color 1** port of the **Mix** map. On the **Noise Parameters** rollout, set **Noise Type** to **Turbulence**, **Levels** to **8.4**, **Size** to **21.2**. Connect a **Noise** map to the **Color 2** port of the **Mix** map. On the **Noise Parameters** rollout, set **Noise Type** to **Turbulence**, **Levels** to **10**, **Size** to **81.5**. On the **Parameter Editor | Mix Parameters rollout**, set **Mix Amount** to **18.4**. Take a test render [Figure 14].

Similarly, create a material for the **floorGeo**. If you want to see the values I have used, open **hoe3_end.max** and check the **floorMat** material.

HOI-4: Creating Rusted Metal Texture

Let's now create a rusted metal texture[see Figure 15]. The summary of tasks you need to complete in this hands-on exercise is as follows:

- Open the start file.
- Create the rust shader.

The following material(s) and map(s) are used in this exercise: **Standard, Composite, Bitmap, Color Correction**, and **Noise**.

Open **hoe4_begin.max** and then press **M** to open the **Slate Material Editor**. In the **Material/Map Browser | Materials | Standard rollout**, double-click on **Standard** to add a **Standard** material to the active view. Rename the material as **rustMat** and apply it to the **Teapot001**. In the **Parameter Editor | Shader Basic Parameters rollout**, check the **2-Sided** check box. Connect a **Composite** map to the **rustMap's Diffuse Color** port using a **Bitmap** map. Now, connect **rust.jpg** to the **Composite** map's **Layer 1** port [see Figure 16]. On the **Parameter Editor | Composite map | Composite Layers | Layer 1 rollout**, click **Add a New Layer** button to add a new layer [see Figure 17]. Notice that a new port with the name **Layer 2** has been added to the **Composite** map node in the active view.

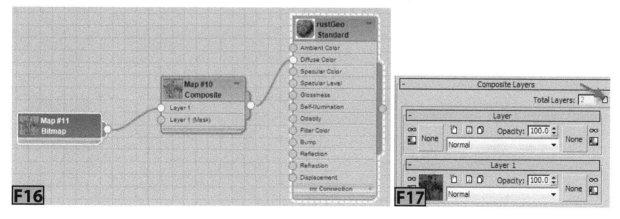

Connect **rustPaint.jpg** to the **Composite** map's **Layer 2** port. On the **Parameter Editor | Composite map | Composite Layers | Layer 2 rollout**, set **Opacity** to **10%** and blend mode to **Color Dodge** [see Figure 18]. Now, take a test render [see Figure 19].

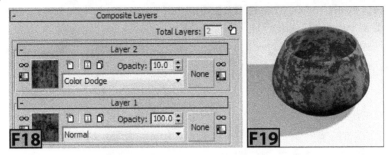

Connect **scratchesMask.jpg** to the **Composite** map's **Layer 2 (Mask)** port using a **Bitmap** map. Now, check the **Invert** checkbox from the **Bitmap's Output** rollout. Take a test render [see Figure 20]. On the **Slate Material Editor's** active view, create copy of the **Bitmap** node connected to the **Composite** map's **Layer 2 (Mask)** node using **Shift**. Connect the duplicate node to the **Bump** node of **rustMat**. On the **Parameter Editor | rustMat | Maps rollout**, set bump map's strength to **10%** and then take a test render [see Figure 21].

Connect a **Noise** map to the **rustMat's Displacement** port. On the **Parameter Editor | Noise map | Noise Parameters rollout**, set **Noise Type** to **Turbulence** and **Size** to **70**. On the **Parameter Editor | rustMat | Maps rollout**, set displacement map's strength to **19%** and then take a test render [Figure 22].

The Last Word

You have learned about different map types in the section B. If you are planning to take your shading and texturing skills to the next level, you will use these maps quite regularly with advanced rendering engine such as mental ray and VRay.

Other Books from Raavi Design

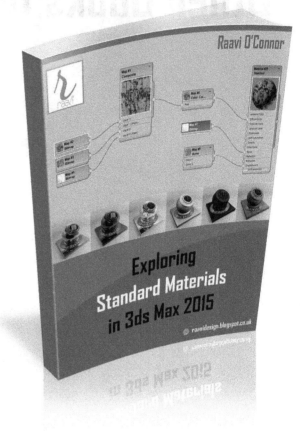

b-2   Other Books by Raavi Design

Raavi O'Connor

Beginner's Guide To
Mental Ray and Autodesk Materials
In 3ds Max 2016

raavidesign.blogspot.co.uk

Raavi O'Connor

Beginner's Guide For
Creating 3D Models
In 3ds Max 2016

raavidesign.blogspot.co.uk

www.ingramcontent.com/pod-product-compliance
Lightning Source LLC
Chambersburg PA
CBHW060507060326
40689CB00020B/4669